Sleeper, Waking
Late Night Reveries at Eighty

ISBN: 979-8-218-04961-4

Cover design: Galen Garwood

Sleeper, Waking
Late Night Reveries at Eighty

PETER WELTNER

Marrowstone Press / Seattle

Night and silence. Who is here?
Weeds of Athens, he doth wear.
    Puck, A Midsummer Night's Dream

How sweet the moonlight sleeps upon this bank!
Here will we sit and let the sounds of music
Creep in our ears: soft stillness and the night
Become the touches of sweet harmony.
    Lorenzo to Jessica, The Merchant of Venice

                Thou hast nor youth nor age,
But, as it were, an after-dinner's sleep,
Dreaming on both.
    The Duke to Claudio in prison, Measure for Measure

Think you there was, or might be, such a man
As this I dreamt of?
    Cleopatra, Antony and Cleopatra

This is the rarest dream that e'er dull sleep
Did mock sad fools withal....
                    I am wild in my beholding.
O heavens bless my girl! But, hark, what music?
    Pericles, Pericles

                The charm dissolves apace,
And as the morning steals upon the night,
Melting the darkness, so their rising senses
Begin to chase the ignorant fumes that mantle
Their clearer reason.

                    We are such stuff
As dreams are made on, and our little life
Is rounded with a sleep.
    Prospero, The Tempest

for Atticus

Robert,

and my sister, Diane

Table of Contents

I. Between Three and Four in the Morning

Migratory 1
A Death in November, from a Distance Apart 3
Eclogue 4
Morning Fog in Winter 5
Called Back: Wright Morris, Stephen Arkin 6
Prophet 8
Orpheus and the Angel of Death 9
Christian 10
Ontologies of Fear 11
Of Waves: after Rhymes on Shelley's Last Lines 13
Bees at Sunrise 14
Sunflowers 16
Halo 17
Restless 18
Gray 19
Ebb and Neap 20
Poetic Forms 21
A Summer Snowstorm 22
Ronnie 23
Gabriel 24
Embarkation 25
Pastoral 26
Sea Birds Gliding in a Sea-Wind 27
Cathedral 28

II. Eight Nights Dreaming

Sunday 31
Monday 32
Tuesday 33
Wednesday 35
Thursday 36
Friday 38
Saturday 39
Sunday 40

III. A Dream Vision Sheaf

1. Dreamers

Jacob 47
Pindar 48
Clytemnestra 51
Virgil 52
St. Paul 53
St. Augustine 54
Xie Lingyun 56
Jianzhang 57
Huineng 58
Caliban 59
Thomas Traherne 60
John Keats 63
Senta 64
Franz Kafka 65
Hart Crane 66
Darl Bundren 67
Thomas Wolfe 69
Antonio Machado 70
Margery Donna Allison 71
Robert Mapplethorpe 72
My Friend Bill 74

2. If Only the Dreamer Could Change the Dream 75

3. Sleepers Awake 83

I

Between Three and Four in the Morning

Migratory

At dawn yesterday, thousands and thousands of birds were
feeding on the beach while the tide receded back
to the sea, leaving behind shallow pools that, blurry
as misty windows, were shadowed by the ashen black
or charcoal gray of the clouds they mirrored.
Pelicans, cormorants, gulls, sandpipers, hundreds
of seabirds blacker than crows piped, chirruped in perfect
pitch. Like silhouettes arrayed where the water ebbs,
glossy, flat as a photograph, no birds stirred. Not even the young
gray hawk perching on a streetlight by The Great Highway
flinched at passing cars, looking for prey as it stared
toward the ocean, talons clutching a road sign. There is a music sung
by birds that's more than their songs, as if their wings were hymns: flapping
as flocks of them suddenly swarm, swirling in the air sonorous as bees buzzing
round a hive, trees rustling before a storm, spinning like a whirlwind, riding the Bay.

Migratory, fearless wanderers,
these birds will soon
be long distance fliers
again, immune
to permanence.
Watch them closely.
They have no solace
to offer, hunger and flight a dance
to no home
to call their own but wind and sea-light. Come
see how they fly as if aspiring to the sun
or play
as they glide and sweep over the beaches. Until their next flight–
tomorrow, tonight,
to the ends of wonder maybe–they'll stay,
feeding, displaying their beautiful need, so long as the anchovy run.

They're gone. All yesterday's migratory birds have left. The tide's coming in or retreating. I can't decide which and would like to believe it is neither. Standing a few yards off from the rock wall of the promontory, rising out of or returning to the sea, as the ocean laps at his waist and chest, Jay beckons me to join him for one last swim. The arc of the sky, just visible through the fog, is his breath, the wind his pulse, the day's impending heat his eyes. My love for him, or my need, is cresting as waves do, breaking hard on the sand, receding back into the ocean. This is my life's one sure solace, what lies in the stillness between low tide and high, where ends and beginnings are ever the same. Let me hunger for what the tides bring in. Which are more beautiful, then (tell me), the birds that leave or those that stay?

A Death in November, from a Distance Apart

—to the memory of Bill Mayer

Whiff the dusky, sweet odor of persimmons fallen
late on the forest floor. A rabbit sniffs the air
through dense shrubbery, alert for predators, men
with ill intent. Two fat gray squirrels do not scare
as a ravenous fox circles their giant tree. Clouds
drift over mountains' rocky cliffs and hillsides,
their massive boulders too craggy to climb. Sweet sounds
of muted voices echo through the valley. A goshawk rides
fast cooling currents like leaves in a breeze. The untold
language of autumn resounds through woods with the silence
that falls after a bell is struck inside an ancient temple where old,
robed monks chant their prayers and slowly retreat into
the litanies of their hibernal solitude, waiting for snow, the end of abundance.
See the geese in their V flying between their habitats? Soon, you'll do
so too, my friend, knowing how tomorrow is too late: the quickening pain, the cold.

Eclogue

I am an old man telling myself your life's story for the last
time and these are the trees you loved in a forest stand,
sap-quickened by sunshine, this the vast
sky that poured its light on the burgeoning land
where you would have lived forever, clinging to earthly things
like lovers clasping hands, if you could have, honey bees
sipping flowers blossoming after mid-spring
showers, wind-tossed petals, leaves unfurling, turtles
basking on rocks, birds singing whatever pleases
them, snakes awakened by sunlight, skittish squirrels
playing their parts in the romance between spring and green boughs,
and I, the old one, a dreamer like the picturesque trees I lie under,
breathing in the cool, sweet air redolent with the scents of May, while you
sleep forever beside me, dreaming, too, of what you'd vowed to remember
always, the stories you told me of the life you'd hoped to have and never knew.

Morning Fog in Winter

A dim aura surrounds the smeared
smudges of oil on pavement.
Like shells
of oysters, shucked and sheared,
the sea is a dappled gray,
its swells
pitted like ice floes.
An invisible
moon glows on the beach,
its dunes shifting,
left unstable
by a wind wailing under its breath.
The ice plants' petals,
orange, peach,
mango, are mist-tipped
with the pallor
of linen shrouds. The hazy blur
of morning fog covers the length
of a shore-
line uncertain
of whether the sun
will shine again
or at last be done
with it,
the circular
voyaging
of its tragic repetitions.

Called Back: Wright Morris, Stephen Arkin

Open one drawer. A pocket watch, its crystal
broken, match book, two bullets, a chain,
a medicine box, a prescription, its ink
blurred and faded, three nickels, two pennies.
Open another. Paper liner from a time long
before: knives, forks, spoons, workaday
utensils, pewter gray, stacked in rows once
neat, now crossed like fallen pick-up sticks.
A curtain between rooms is thin as an old
wedding veil, a rocker barely visible behind
the lace, brass tacks securing its upholstery.
An oval mirror reflects the knob on the door.
Is anyone at home? Or are these just things?
I look with you, Steve. An old clock stuck at five after. A last light
shining from an antique oil lamp, its chimney hands clasped in prayer.

Or in yet another photograph, it's the Home Place,
Wright's Uncle Harry entering a barn through
a door black as the back of a mirror, black
as the shed where his useless Model T is stored,
the door frame surrounding him pitted by weather
and time, the clapboard even more worn, an ancient
tin pail lying on its side in the dust-bowl-
dry-sandy soil while Harry, wearing his railroad
cap and a faded, torn jacket, his shoulders drooping
after a long life's labors, steps into the unknown
dark before him like someone oppressed by
an unseen light, cloud heavy in a cloudless sky. Listen.
Hear it, Steve? The prairie still blows mercilessly through these
scenes, creaking swings, slamming shutters, tumbleweed crackling
like fireballs over a cracked earth stricken by depression and drought.

The territory ahead. "L'essence du visible" was
the title of the show in Paris of Wright Morris'
work you helped to prepare in the years
before your death. The essence of the visible.
In your introduction to its catalogue, you wrote,
in French, that when Wright Morris saw the effects
of time on buildings it had left broken, in ruins,
the furniture it had damaged, the intimate things
of life it had cast aside he also found, somehow,
by the grace of photography, writing, his way
home, to the spare world where his people lived,
the things they'd left behind them after their deaths,
like the garden a young Wright wandered in Vienna
where the blind roamed confined by walls for their safety,
smelling scents, touching petals unstirred by winds, even in storms,

the roses pruned to remove all danger of thorns,
the slate walkway square and regimented
to protect them from falling. So Viennese. So
European like the man he had met who chose
to wear women's clothes to transform the violence
besieging him into a preternatural calm. Yet home
called Wright back despite the daily mourning
of those who had stayed there, the Nebraska plains
infinite as oceans, the trees bare as mail boxes,
spare as the poles they perched on, where a train
passing through scratched a smudged pencil line
across the horizon while the boy he was performed
his chores under broad-shouldered shadows, gathering eggs,
chipping shit off chicken wire, as if life has a way of always calling
us back, Steve, if not to home exactly, then somewhere else no one leaves.

Prophet

A sick crow drags its limp right wing on the street,
at each step it takes croaks a clacking, slow
rattle like knocking on wood blocks. Its feet
are scaly as snake skin, a bird out of Poe,
that scared. It cannot hop, but struts one foot
after the other like an old man, wobbly
as he walks, fearful that he'll fall. Its soot
black feathers are dusted with ash and sea-
salt. It is headed for the park, for trees with low
branches and lots of shade to rest under.
There it will wait. Who knows how much time
it has left to live? It has lost its flock. A murder
of crows, some call it. Let me acknowledge it as mine,
this thing of darkness. Let me learn all that it knows
about dying. The night it would fly to at the end of the mystery.

Orpheus and the Angel of Death

"A long sustained slow chant," said Stravinsky
of his score. Instead of Orpheus' lyre, a harp is played
over the sonority
of winds, a walking bass lines, the music's parade
of rhythms, crystalline colors. The strings,
near the piece's end, intone a mournful "sul
ponticello," as if to sing of serious things,
of tragedy, of how cruel
fate can be until, finally, the horns
play a fugue that sounds like a litany,
like an apotheosis. If Orpheus no longer mourns
where goats nibble on hills by trees where creeks flow
but dwells in some other world far away as the sun
at its zenith in heaven, you who would go
to Hades to rescue Persephone, Eurydice,
or Zagreus twice over, too, must hear in his music how the journey's begun.

We all live in the same moment forever, Balanchine
said. There is no future, no past. His is an Orphic
art that claims all lost times are our time
now. In his ballet, Death entices Orpheus and his music
to go with him to Hades,
dancing, as they descend, a pas de deux like enemies
apart, lovers entwined. Who grieves
for their loss more, Eros or Thanatos? Whose lyric
impulses soar higher
than the sun, Death's or Orpheus'?
Their bodies strong, taut, in tune with mask and lyre,
they dance their defiance. In the wildest places
of the heart, in a fabled, Dionysian Thrace,
say, the Angel of Death woos Orpheus for his music, his artifice.
Which is what mourning sometimes is. A love that tricks death with its magic.

Christian

I remember when you first noticed Christian as he passed by
you as he strolled down Fifth Avenue. Like many others,
you stumbled into a tree, cursing yourself for stupidly
tripping, then crashed into the park's stone wall. Lovers
of men do dumb things when drunk on looks. Who'd
guess you'd stalk him at the MET, gazing at the same
time as he did at a black figure vase? When you could,
you'd sit near him at the Oak Room when he came
in to drink with friends or patrons. That era's long past,
sweetheart, for us, too. In his photos, Christian is the most
handsome man who has ever lived. Such allure should last
forever but seldom does. It's only longing that is never lost.
See? Christian bumps into you again on Seventy First near Madison.
He wants you. Every man we knew then is still alive. And beautiful. And alone.

Ontologies of Fear

1

Each person now alive mirrors someone who has died
or is yet to be born. Walking through museum
galleries I might find in time, if the past has not lied,
a portrait of a face familiar as my own, the sum
of who I am. Or in every crowded theater
I might spy a head like an ancient noble's
carved in stone. Yes. I know. Time is a river.
I've eighty years to show it's so. Snapshots plagiarize.
Photos reveal ghosts. 'Now' and 'Then' are doubles
of each other. And the future finds the bodies
it desires waiting to duplicate mine or yours.
Every story told repeats itself. Life's fine old lies
are heard each day. And every dream dreamed recurs
and, obscure as an oracle, prophesies who lives, who dies.

2

The earth steams, the sky grows misty. A black cloud rumbles.
I pick berry sprigs for luck. Cicada chirr, flies
and bees buzz, tree frogs croak, throb. My troubles
begin anew as birds, twittering, spin melodies
to tell of storms to come. Yet my day is lovely
still. Woods provide a cave I can feel safe in when
the thunderstorm rages through. I am content, happy
in wilderness. "Life turns pearls to tears. Women,
men alike were innocent like you once," my teacher
said to warn me. Forsythia, butterfly bushes shade me
as I lie by wild roses that cling to a fence. I pick a flower
free of its petals. Three cardinals clutch a pine limb as pollen,
glimmering, swirls in the air. A hound brays at a rising moon's silver
light as birds flap their wings to beat back night from hearts, dark and unforgiven.

3

Peach, apple blossoms fall into my lap. Remember that?
I shook them off, stood up. A stray dog, maybe
wild, rustled through bushes chasing a feral cat
or possum. The rain quit at dawn. Wander with me.
Listen to the birds as they return to chirruping
and chatter as I sit on a boulder watching
a river overflowing its banks. Try to ponder
how a child, a fearful boy might find water
to be a ceaseless mystery. Change and flux and transience.
I grab the branch of a sycamore that has fallen
during a storm, climb on its moss-covered trunk
while the sun glares through thin low clouds. My conscience
shines like that, bright, piercing, and unrelenting. I should have sunk,
drowned, when I jumped. I've told you why before. And swore I'd do it again.

4

Dreams are parables of childhood fears I who write
about them do not understand. As crows performed
dances on a circular, bare patch at night
on the floor of impenetrable woods, I imagined
them moving unseen with the grace of a hummingbird
beating its wings as it feeds or a hawk that flies
in spiraling flight to snatch its prey, its cries unheard.
Darker than evening, crows prance, dance in the guise
of who knows what other birds even as they
clack their beaks and sing of joys they'd never
known with gritty voices, parched as sand,
and sway to winds flowing with the force of water.
Dreams in old age are like woods at night when, though I've planned
to be in a bed, I'll watch birds dark as darkness dancing, free as child's play.

Of Waves: after Rhymes on Shelley's Last Lines

If madness 'tis to be unlike the world,

it is also to find no comfort in larks at sunset, in ocean air,
or to take no pleasure in morning, in a first ray
of sunlight folded between crags in a boulder, there

for a moment, then gone for good. It is to look only the tragic way,
backward, to the past, to confront the cold countenance
of history staring hostilely at you by night and day,

to be blind to a lover's smiles, the grace of a stranger's glance.
No one can really remember the lives of those who have died
before them. Who could bear always having to dance

with the dead, entranced by their ghostly music? Wayside
of any path we have traveled, even the future has passed
us by. On a beach near where swimmers have drowned, rocks abide

outside of time, each like an epitaph on a tombstone ordered cast
by survivors. Though storms, tides, have rolled
over them for centuries, they have endured on this shore, will last

long as the cliff they've fallen from, stones piled for those lost in the fold
of

Bees at Sunrise

The salty air stings my eyes.
A boy has risked high waves,
and drowned. On a rung

of a rescue ladder, a fireman tries
to spot him. He was a strong
kid, but the Pacific craves

strength. The tide carried his body
southerly, below where
the crew was searching. A chopper

circles above the sea so noisily
it mutes a scream. The water
froths with foam as its blades tear

at the crests. Once evening's begun,
the crowded beach
empties, the search

done. One dawn, decades ago,
as I watched dozens
of bees buzzing in our garden's

patch of indigo
and black eyed susans
and feeding, steady and slow,

on nectar, I knew it'd be over
soon, our last summer
of folly, you whom I'd miss

as no other,
your looks so much like his
in the paper I am reading,

the drowned kid none
would doubt I am weeping for
while you stand again by the door

to our garden, opening
it once more
for me before you leave,

to see how beautiful you are
as you grieve,
how calm this morning's ocean.

Sunflowers

After a break in the clouds, a plait of blue
sky caresses a field of golden sunflowers,
the air translucent and watery. I believed you
even as I tried not to count the hours
I'd lain sleepless recalling a small snail I once
saw slipping through my father's garden
on its slick belly as a cat prepared to pounce
on it. Why must children's hearts harden?
Everyone should love the world before they leave
it, at least once. Light showers, a field of sunflowers,
and a sky by noon bluer even than a blue jay's
feathers as it flies past me who would likely grieve
for the lives of everything alive, my father says
too sensitive to survive, knowing how one thing devours
another. And the morning I woke to you, the sunflowers facing
east as if in obeisance to your radiance in bed beside me, sun-warm and golden.

Halo

His friend will soon be safely out of other's sight,
though restless for morning,
the trees' sprite-
like icicles, crackling,
glittering like fireflies in summer. It would please
him to speak of the things
he keeps secret, the guy he's just made love to,
the lanyard necklace, the copper rings
he'd made for him, but hid in a drawer. Nothing's true
about his life anymore. The boy flew
away early, when the clock
chimed eleven. Through his window, the moon shocks
him, like the happiness that comes as a surprise
in the midst of a hallowed night, the glowing aura around it, blue,
yellow, rust, and cerise.

Restless

Even as he sleeps, he can still hear
the heady
throbbing of frogs
in drying ponds,
so near
he is to their catastrophe.
Hickory trees
webbed with caterpillar
tents
and wild rose
thickets
thrive roadside,
sparkling,
kissed by dew like
a lover's eyes at first light.

No locusts drone
in the frizzled
grass,
no thunder rumbles
through the sky.
A black beetle inches
up a window screen.
None know the woods
he crosses
every night
through tangled stalks
of milkweed, goldenrod, sumac
to anywhere west
of sunrise,
where night lingers on and on.

Gray

Today, the clouds that fill the sky are pale gray
like thin, wet snow on stones. The sea's
the gray of tarnished tin cans. Let the day
be what I mean. Let gray weather seize
the soul that sees it. Sailing westward,
a cargo ship looks pencilled in,
surfers in wet suits tiny as ink spots. Toward
the north, mist obscures the hills like rain.
The froth from waves is gray as an old sheet.
The sand is a brownish gray like timber
stripped and tossed aside. A gray sleet
falls on the seawall and the slick icy water.
This is a day that promises no meaning. Tomorrow,
somewhere far away, he'll trace a herd of gray whales
migrating to new feeding grounds as each exhales
the geyser-like spouts that will shine everyday in the sun like a rainbow.

Ebb and Neap

I watch waves break and break
on the beach, letting me know about
time, how it repeats for the sake
of the rhythm in things, in our lives. Out
of necessity, we learn how sorrow
is part of love, pity
the beginning of compassion. Tomorrow,
the waves will say to me,
"You are old. Let the dead bestow
their gifts, voices, ancient stories,
eternal patterns of change." Below
my feet, I sense in the threatened shoreline,
the presence of something divine,
lost, buried deep in the earth, waiting to rise again in glory.

Poetic Forms

Waves collapse while fighting each other,
riptides clash, like the futility of wars pent-
up in nature. A plover
picks at a bed of kelp. I went
away for a while. To wait. New storms
loom in the clouds as the sea
opens to the sky like flowers,
craving more light. Poetic forms
are the shapes indwelling in things, ours
to save and cherish. Let it be so: what we believe
but can't say, rhythm not the beat
of a pulse but the movement of wind,
the music of words what one cannot survive
without. Waves clash and vanish, yet how sweet
the day is as if somewhere in poetry all of creation were still alive.

A Summer Snowstorm

It is summer in the Bay's season-free world,
one day wintery cold, the next
autumn hot as if weather means to purge
us of how we mark time, as perplexing

as it would be in Eden before the fall,
no day logically following another.
I remember when I was small,
playing outside in the middle of summer

how astonished I was by the snow as it fell,
the hour, day, season suspended
in the white of December, the smell
of Christmas thick in the air. It was said

the snow had come from mountains
three hundred miles to our west
that blizzard winds blew hard as rains
in an August thunderstorm as if, at the behest

of an unknown power, it meant to astound us, after-
wards everything clothed in white as my father,
mother, sister, and I stood together
gazing at our first glimpse of paradise, silenced by wonder.

Ronnie

Mine is the music of birds, stray dogs, squirrels,
locust I hear at twilight after a storm,
of a creek coursing slowly into the lake
near my home while the moon, crescent or full,

rises like a voyager on a familiar journey
over water, its pale light broken
by rippling waves into thousands
of silvery fragments, fish-scales shiny,

and the stars the lake brightly mirrors
glittering like gold coins spewed
from the loins of constellations,
while below the stone dam the swirling

currents murmur sighs, lamentations
apprehended only by nocturnal woods
and maybe, oh, I don't know,
the lords of the world and all its waters,

divinities, ghosts in the night, I see better
the more I grow sleepier, the clouds
hovering outside my windows defining
the shadows of tall trees and houses that seem

to be drowning far below the lake's tenebrous
surface where I nightly swim deep
underwater amid the reeds and eelgrass
trying to find my friend who early that morning

had stripped to dive in, swimming, treading
water, drying his body by sunning naked
while he lay on a grassy bank: a reverie that each time I look
at it grows more lasting, like words we pray for the past's sake.

Gabriel

I think of the dawn he and I spied a moth's golden
wings dangling from a spider web as tightly woven
through brush twigs as the cat's cradle he threaded
later for me between his slim deft fingers as we lay in bed.
while the cicadas' rasping thickened the air
and a red-eyed possum gaped at us. Fireflies flickered
on screens, skirting bushes. We pushed our bed closer
to the window, lay naked on a naked mattress, dared
the days ahead to be better than ours were then.

Nights were an underground tunnel, an underground
cave, a hole we hid in. Bat cry, owl cry, the cries
of stray dogs. Leaves rustling.
                                        Like gold I'd found,
I see the hairs on your arms glistening. Who
dies for no reason at seventeen?
                                        We're playing cards.
listening to 45s lying side by side or to the radio
as we brag about the lives we'll have made for ourselves
some day, how everything will turn out fine, what's hard
rendered easy. And you say, out of nowhere, "All will be well
when time is good to our kind,"

                    as if you knew more then than I do now, Gabriel.

Embarkation

No more troop ships embark from here to carry soldiers
to war. The piers' rickety pilings are slowly rotting
into the bay. No more anxious families, fearful lovers
wave their last goodbyes. Tonight, the moon's shining
too glaringly to sleep by. I brood on the past, of words
I wish I'd never heard spoken. In old mariners' stories,
some sailors never stop sailing, denied both worlds,
the deep sea and land. In tales of their fate, time weaves
its mysteries. I was to meet you here when the fighting
had ended, you freed by peace to come home. But war
is like a wharf to nowhere, the dying sighs of water lapping
against piles, the creaking of decaying docks: a metaphor
(not mine, but history's) for all that has died within us. Waves
may roar louder, cities fall, bombs blast, fires rage, but what saves
us from disasters? I stare into the night, as if it gave light, like a ship
signaling its way back to harbor.

Pastoral

Clouds, mountains, trees mirrored by a lake,
but not inverted to trees, mountains, clouds.
The water reflects waves that break
like an avalanche, a tsunami that astounds
with its power, worse than bad weather.
Skies that appear to threaten no harm,
that over hills look like a safe summer storm,
are seen on a Marin lake to hide a nether
world. Hills, grass, trees welcome the rain,
but look below. Waves churn up the dark stain
that taints all things. The lake is to blame,
clouds, hills, trees seen through the same
mirror as your eyes see your face in. Let it tell
you why this world as it is is the same world that fell.

What if God had caught the earth in his arms as it fell?
Embraced us, too? What stories of him would we tell?
A man, maybe me, circles a lake in Marin, the same
lake I'd been hiking for weeks, searching. Who'd blame
me? I long to see him again, hunkering, the stain
of sweat on his t-shirt, his hair wet from rain,
his hands cupped to drink. I'm afraid of the nether
world, another nightmare waking me up. A new storm
stirs behind the hills. He looks hungry. What harm
would it do? I hand him my sandwich. The weather
is changing to spring. The man winks, astounds
me with his smile. The sun is about to break
through. He strips, swims away. Light as light, clouds,
hills, trees float away as he drifts out of memory, to nowhere on a glassy lake.

Seabirds Gliding in the Sea-Wind

Sleek Brandt's cormorants, a lone black-footed albatross,
dozens of ravens dark as the charred driftwood littering
the beach, gulls, some whiter than the light-polished gloss
that glows off porcelain or the sparkling crests of breaking
waves, others sandy brown, the flat gray of pewter or slate:
hosts of seabirds gliding in the sea-wind over a sea
that today is the grayish-green-blue of moss-covered granite,
each bird looping, circling, drifting down, rarely
flapping its wings, then lifted higher as if to inhabit
wherever currents carry it, borne further upward
by first light even more than by the fierce winds blowing
in landward off the Pacific. Then suddenly all of them, as in a fable,
vanish together, disappear who knows where, as if transported toward
an uncharted island like explorer's ships in old stories in squalls, wind-tossed
and lost the moment I woke up, as if scattered on an atoll, safe, faraway, and invisible.

Cathedral

All the west is a shiny mottled gray this morning, the shore
silvery as grains of shale while the subdued waves
attempt no more than chalky low crests. Flat as a floor,
the sea looks poured from cement and gravel. The day's
just beginning, the sun, delayed over eastern hills,
pale as candle light flaming behind a gauze
curtain. A wall of fog, sheer as rocky cliffs, fills
the sky for miles across the horizon. Like a pause
in time, like a glimpse of eternity, a solitary cloud
of mist hovers over the Pacific, a sheet or a scrim
illuminated by dawn as if the fog were endowed
with a corporeal presence, a radiance waiting to be born.
As a breeze blows east, it's haunting, inviting as a hymn
I loved as a boy in a church I'd stand outside, feeling torn
whether I should enter it or not, believe in it or not, submit to its worship.

As yet no cruiser, no fishing boats, not a single cargo ship
coasts along the shoreline. No birds fly skyward this morning.
But by evening, returning, sunset will burn a golden red
in a crackling wind, fog-free for half an hour or more, gilding
the breasts of cormorants, gulls gliding, soaring ahead
of the dark, their feathers sparkling like amethysts. At Land's
End, the bluffs behind me will blaze with the intensity
of raw steel molten in foundry furnaces. Ribbons, bands
of yellow, orange, and red will unfurl in the heavens. The sea
will turn lotus-blue again, the waves, peaking, will be tinted
with gold, the loose sand on the beach scatter freely as pollen
wind-tossed over the land, as if seeding new life. And as a raven
struts on driftwood or preens, content, blacker than a newly frocked
priest, I will keep watch on the west as the end of dusk glows as it does sometimes
as if from within a cathedral's rose-colored windows while night's bell tower chimes.

II

Eight Nights Dreaming

Sunday

A shallow creek, a peaceful lake
in the park, squirrels, songbirds, meadows.
The smell of baking bread, of fresh flowers
in crystal vases on the table by the foyer.
The whirr of her sewing machine. She's making
a new dress. In our backyard, by willows,
Mother unbraids her hair. Hours
pass free as her laughter.
Sitting in her swing.
Or a morning on the green.
The town's streets and square,
earth, sky, all I'd seen,
my people kind and fair:
why old men live by dreaming.

Monday

You'll never know how many dreams I've dreamed about you.

Once you've left it, youth's a country you can't renew or return
to. Old friends are living elsewhere, too, or have died while you
were away. Roads, streets you shouldn't need maps to learn
freshly are a maze, your town no longer the refuge you knew

but a labyrinth with no end to it, like woods you'd roamed in freely,
eager to get lost in, that scare you now, pathless and pitch-dark.
Remember how I'd park the car, lights out, by the lake to see
how long it'd take before you'd hold my hand? A horned lark,

a killdeer, a robin might be singing before I'd drive you home.
Or the motel, the smell of mildew on the sheets, in the shower,
five dollars an hour, off Route 401, the coffee in styrofoam
mugs? I should have found us a cleaner place to hide in. Or safer.

I traveled further than you ever could, tried to meet you somewhere
alone on my few trips back, both still young, in our early twenties.
But you'd married. Fantasies, like the mist breath makes in cold air,
the winter wedding I'd missed, my unwritten letters, unspoken pleas.

The slow rural road your family's house sat by has become
a busy highway. No loves are greater than those old age makes up,
the cows drowsing near us as we took our first brave sips of rum
mixed with RC cola I'd carefully pour into our shared paper cup.

Your fingers touch my face, trace my lips. Who pays the greater price,
the one who leaves or the one who stays? Wasted days are a crime
against youth, but lost years like to dream. Kiss me once, then kiss me twice,
then kiss me once again. It's been a long, long time.

Tuesday

It is the wide-awake that saves
us from fantasy, not night
nor half-lit shadows of dusk
or dawn, but a soul yearning

for morning to come, birds
aloft in the soft air of first light,
cars on streets, highways,
people crowding buses

and sidewalks, hurrying to work,
nocturnal dreams set aside,
ignored, forgotten,
distracted by the usual day,

the fascinations of the commonplace.
It is the reasonable tragedy
most suns wake us to,
an ordinary suffering.

Back to me, a boy stands
at a bank's window–blond,
tall, lovely–staring at me
staring at him, ruining his reflection.

I saw him just that once.
I imagine him dead now
like one of Job's blessed
sons Jahweh failed to revive.

It hurts how the dead won't
stay dead, the forgotten
forgotten just because
it's easier to see them at night,

the past more real in dreams.
It is always like that.
You begin to come
back to me. I reach out

to touch you. It rains.
A bird lands on my window
still beating its wings,
frantic to get in. It's winter.

It should have flown south
but forgot to. I cannot
change my dream to save
it. I want you. I want you.

Wednesday

A child, a child
dreaming of loss, of being
without parents,

abandoned, free, wants nothing
more than to be who he is,
happy in the wild

places he lives in at night,
asleep, a bird on the wing
without belongings,
just seeing all the air brings
with the wind,
like a starling or a blue jay flying

freely. Night's expansive starlit heavens,
the sky's clarity
on a cloudless day,
and the boy I am I dream of
using the wide lens
of a magnifying glass

and sun's rays on decaying
leaves to make them burn,
the wind blowing

ashes into the sky
where all things
he'd set on fire would go.

Thursday

The screen is too wide to take it all in
in one view.
No matter how far back you stand,
the mountains,

like gigantic moss-covered
pine cones, lean,
look to be bent askew
by time and wind,

their slopes too sheer
to hike. Move
from panel to panel.
So much is shown

in miniature–minuscule cranes,
two men poling
two tiny boats
and a thin river slightly widening

as it flows west–that you think,
culture, a civilization,
tradition, means this:
life intensified, movement stilled.

A solitary duck floats
downstream.
High up, in a wood hut,
two men,

in fluent robes, talk, gesturing,
their aged faces
little more than a few,
quick brush strokes.

In a den of sorts, not quite the mouth
of a cave, a monk sits,
praying, shaded by clouds
and a plum tree trunk.

Turn around. A porcelain bowl
displayed in a case
behind thick glass,
is white like robes worn to mourn

a passed soul, pure
as a jade vase
vast age has not changed
save for a swirl

of pale blue around
a thin inner rim–
an almost flat pot,
or dish, silent, cold as frost.

Some day it will come, like
a blunt moment
of shock, spirits appearing
while you sleep. A new

bowl, whiter than fresh snow
but old in its devotions,
like a monk praying in a cave
dreaming of the ghosts that moulded it.

Friday

Its dream is tonight's winds blowing the world westward, the ever changing sea and sky.

It is a play enacted by others, its plot unfolding toward some surprising happy ending.

It is these white spumes tossed by an incoming storm across the beach while plovers skitter on sand feeding on larvae.

It is water flowing through gutters, down drains, across the sand rushing toward the sea with nothing to lose or gain.

It is my mind as it wanders, lost in dreaming dreams of rollers roaring in, of three crows cawing in shrill reply,

the hurts and wounds I sleep to, the gulls' cries I hear at night, a flock of them on a long winter journey,

restless as waves under a cloud-muted sun, knowing how mortally cold the Pacific is, how many souls it has undone,

how all travelers yearn to be returned to port, like dreamers back from sleep.

Saturday

This is me dreaming of reading
The Tempest
for the last time.
This is a tree, the lone survivor
of a stand,
sap-saddened by solitude, the loss,
the contrast
it knows between then and now,
the desolate land
to which its roots cling like fingers
losing their grip.
No birds nest in its spindly limbs.
No skittish
squirrels climb its peeling bark.
Its bole is infected
with canker, gnarled and pitch black.
No longer do bees
sip its blossoms. No more do
petals rain
on girls and boys below.
The romance
of its boughs, dreamers of the shade
they hid in,
an apple grove's scents in August,
the bed-soft
soil, redolent of fall, of the day
the children
will return to savor its fruit.
This is a tree
that has been hymned by all seasons.
This is Ariel
leaving it. This is at last its last winter
praising it,
the dream that ends all dreaming
in the victory of sleep.

Sunday

The wind calms at first light. It is a seasonable
cold this morning. The tide is out, a lull
beachside after yesterday's storm. Dawn is a tale
of hills where the sun is delayed, of a full

moon that appears to be suspended
mythically in the sky, a radiance to it
as it lolls above the sea as if illuminated
by more than the sun, like a globe lit

from within. It is easy for a body to move
through the world when the air is so still,
so raptly quiet. Is there a light above
the sun's that some days decides to fill

the earth with splendor? Wood scents pass
freely through it, eucalyptus' wet bark,
Douglas fir's, redwood's, the grass,
sea oats, the fern trees in the park,

their resiny, pungent smells keener by day.
No crows are cawing, no songbirds singing.
What I'm seeing is like theater, a silent play
I've stepped into, a moon that's never setting.

One pale dawn follows another, the steady
rains winter-heavy, the gutters on each street
clogged with brown leaves. Then, abruptly,
skies clear. Forsythia, jasmine compete

with gardenia, magnolia, camellias, azaleas,
jonquils, dogwood, red and snow white roses,
all blooming freely, their iridescent petals
flouting drab rules or whatever imposes

its cold order on nature. A garden, long
left to tend itself, is reviving. Spring birds
fly back, their songs mingling in one song
orioles, thrushes, chickadees. Tiny herds,

like cartoons, of squirrels, chipmunks scurry about
the yards, chattering, playing on trees,
showing what it means to be devout,
to see through your eyes what May sees.

So far north, June shocks as in a Russian
novel. First winter thaws in shadows. Raw
mud turns grass's emerald. Then the land
flares into the Chinese colors I saw

as the sun shone through crane-white clouds
on an ancient silkscreen, a priest, plain,
hog-fat, sucking plums, making no sounds,
quieter than lotus on the mountain. Plums stain

his robe wine-red. A boat waits by his hut.
In farewell, he embraces the farmer who hoes
his beds, its flowers topaz, agate.
If beauty's found in decay, winter snows,

in labor, the raked-over loam, the icy gate,
then summer's dreams are paradisal. By stone
walls and cliffs, his skiff flows. Rice, dates
fill his bowl and plate. Peace comes to everyone.

III

A Dream Vision Sheaf

1. Dreamers

Jacob

Perhaps this is what Jacob saw. His old ladder.
No angelic crowds climbing up and down it.
Just a way to see night's onset better,
the ribbons of gauzy clouds in a sky lit
by twilight floating over head, stunning
his sight like silvery strips of tin mirroring
a sun shining brightest as it fades. A solitary
star is burning up the sky, fiery as a meteor.
He climbs up his tall step ladder to see
it clearer, amazed how, like a chunk of gold ore
just mined from the earth, it glows in the sky
with a luminosity fiercer than the moon's,
far bolder than any star he has seen before.
Imagine its light were an angel possessing
a god-like strength Jacob wrestles with, communes
with, a seraph disguised as a star early rising
into Jahweh's endless day, now in his dream life just beginning.

Pindar

1

Mt. Tamalpais,
too green for Greece yet
god-lit,

a dream of a strange peace
on fire in the sunset
behind it,

a goat cart
in my ears as I watch
children play-

ing at the start
of evening, two boys catch-
ing in their hands the last light of day.

2

Wind-, fog-drenched, not rain
but mist dazzling, cool-
ing late morning,

a beach where, see, again
boys like us in a tide pool
idly wading.

3

Summer weather
in Carolina fifty five
years ago,

or today, here, where it is hotter,
less clear, alive
with tourists, no

thunderstorms mid-aft-
ernoon, no fireflies
at evening

as at twilight back home, we two laugh-
ing, counting how many, your sighs
more joyful than anything.

4

Like wind to sails, blue
skies to sun, boys as young
as we, not yet men,

concealing nothing, yet not quite true
either, speechless, like a tongue
on fire with all it burns unspoken.

5

Your skin after swimming like oil
on a naked wrestler
in heroic Greece,

youth unspoil-
ed by fear. The epic matter
of hair like gold fleece.

6

Though no Greek poet,
of course, I would pray
to the sea,

horizon, unbro-
ken sky, "May you stay
forever by me."

7

Waves unerringly
roar, the Pacific I
walk beside

daily, ocean older than memory
now at its high-
est known tide,

a sea ancient as Homer's, no
less wild, vast, dan-
gerous to

voyage on, to be betrayed by: not you
but him, long ago, racing through rain
to someone new.

8

Whoever catches the bright glances
flashing from Theoxenus'
eyes

is tossed into the fast rising wild seas
of his desires (discus
thrower, gymnast). Whoever denies

his infatuation, lies that he dreams
of him by night
and day possesses a heart of stone,

more adamant than iron, how he gleams
with oil, like this paean I write
to a god, bereft, alone,

the beauty, you remember, whose Dorian
sandals I'd once fitted for
his dance of splendor,

along with the garlands Pindar placed on Theron's
royal brow, to adore
him solely, braided olive shoots for crown.

Clytemnestra

In the Peloponnesus, in Mycenae, try to imagine the stone walls,
iron gates, gold masks, hidden bronze doors now lost
to history, its palace's narrow, ghost-haunted halls,
cliffs behind it where water poured off rock frost-
pale in the morning cold, and the enormous marble fountain
that bore purifying water from the sacred mountain
whose hillsides hid the spirits of those who had died
among its sacred leaves, vines, and outcrops hazy
in the mist at dawn.
                                        Agamemnon will die, too. He's lied,
her husband, from kingly pride all his cruel life.
                                                                                                    Yet Clytemnestra's baby,
her sole son, last night was a coiling snake she tried
to feed with her breast. But it bit her and curdled
her milk. Her scream as she woke at once alerted
her sleeping guards.
                                        Guilty dreams fly into and out of her mind
auspicious as hawks'. Orestes will return soon to find
her terrified of his strong arm and sword. Serpentine, oneiric furies, ophidian
venom are the children you bore for tragedy, for Clytemnestra.
                                                                                                                                The nightmare
of dying at the hands of your only son.

Virgil

The bough the tree gives me, the path down that the ground
traces for me, the guide his poem is for me, the photos
in it, the grove that lights my way as if its leaves
shine like torches, the cave's mouth, the haunting sound
of long absent voices whispering, the spirit that glows
from ghosts like twilight in woods, their tears, what grieves
deepest under earth or in an echoing grotto, the city,
the people Aeneas lost, Troy's forests chopped, toppled,
his last glimpse of it burning, crackling, in his head
its buildings still on fire, courthouse, school, steeple,
the new world he creates over the sea, the city he'd battled
to stay in now in ruins like the shades who have said
to him by wind-gnawed craters: History is a disaster,
for even the living must wander as restless as water,
must flicker like those in subterranean caverns, unfree,
every name erased by rain and wind from every gravesite,
he who can't know in the days to follow what might
befall him save missing the friends death has taken
from him, and I no Aeneas, no hero, unsure of my future, with no Rome,
no city, no family to honor me–seeking after them, wanting them home
at least in memory, in the house where I live grown old by restless seas,
the men, the lovers the plague stole from me, my dreams of them, their untold stories.

St. Paul

Envision it. The body in love embodies the body of love.
The body lives inside the soul. Record what you might know of
it. A small beach, its gritty sand brittle as dry grass. A lake,
rippling through reeds, slapping against a cement pier
beneath a diving board. A solitary garter snake.
Jasmine. Magnolia. Roses. Their perfumes belong here
with us now. Houses' lights flickering off the calm water
that mallards drift on sleepily. White sheets of clouds
veiling a waxing moon. A dam, its overflow stirring
the quiet creek below it. What nighttime enshrouds
a dream revives. A car door slammed. The humid air
dew-heavy. His naked body like mirrored light, the glow
off gold, the patina on bronze. An August late night is smiling
down upon us with its usual enticements. What two boys dare
do by loving. Eyes that meet in secret and know why. So
it is not paradise, maybe never. Yet call it grace. The shock of new beginnings.

St. Augustine

1

Yours is a metaphysical pain born of chastisement. Or a strange grace. Their feet
like dancers, weighty, arched to float skyward despite their muscularity,
their garments thistle blue, rose rust, angels gaze
down upon you less in angelic horror than mystified by
what humanity must endure, as if it does not faze
them quite, winged as they are, to have seen how easily flesh suffers its defeats.

They see, as well, how rapt your mother is, and your friend, who stare down
from somewhere impossible to behold. Look. Look anyplace around you.
In forests or farmlands. On the sea. In every village, town,
or city. Consider the ordinary sorrows people daily suffer through
their losses. A father in a bedroom where his dying son sleeps, so dear
to him he cannot bear it. An old woman who does know
that soon she must leave her life. I should tell you, too, of a lover lying on a gurney
long
ago
lacerated by Kaposi's, his blind eyes lit brighter than yours, Augustine, intensified by
fear.

2

Honeysuckle, thornless roses basking under a midday sun, the shade cool as twilight's
shadows. A child is a memory of peace, sometimes, like the pages between the covers
of a book sufficing to keep them from harm, guarded by their bindings.

Mist at dusk as dust specks float among spiky spruce needles, oak leaves that prickle
the slick surface of a pond where a sleek, slithering king snake burrows into loamy
black earth, wild roses, tiger lilies, blue flag irises proliferating like reeds on its banks,
while
clouds sail like ships toward home and harbor.

The secrets a garden keeps should sustain a boy in faith forever, but he betrays it anyway. Milkweed suppurating sap. Green lynx spiders. Preying mantises devouring crickets. Viridescent streams. Days emerald as his birthstone, a spring as verdant as his youthful dreams. I mean green in the sense of unknowing, of green things dreamily remembering, all that would keep him from needing to be elsewhere.

Pink and white dogwood, freshly trimmed boxwood emit an electric charge into the air sharp as ice. Then a sudden rain falls amid northern breezes, pungent as teakwood.

Is this, this imaginary garden, possibly the source of Augustines's dreams, his vision of every Eden's paradisal reality?

3

And still higher we soared, Augustine writes, flying inwardly as marvels poured down on us. And so their presence pierced our souls, my mother's and my friend's as well, elevating us beyond ourselves, like sacred scrolls meant to be read allegorically if one wishes to discern a dream's hidden meanings:

that we might reach, touch invisibility, even if this time I failed to, even if I recoiled at such majesty, the unendurable wisdom out of which all things are created, the sum of eternity.

If He wills it, let past, present, future return me to my mere human speech, my impure language, unsure of the efforts of my heart when left alone, yet no more a part of the transient world anymore, but belonging to my dreams, where unspoken words and mysteries begin and end.

I would seek again what I by myself could not have apprehended because I am a sinner from birth and remain too worldly a thinker, too easily spent by the strength of the vision that would give my life meaning. Let night light my way again. Let me dream such a beautiful dream again.

Let me comprehend each of its meanings and heed the words that would show me how to tell you of them. Let me name the place I've seen. Let life and poetry be one and the same.

Xie Lingyun

All through the village, by water's strict
edges, people suffer. The age of Three
Great Griefs promises no end. Joy
darkens eyes with its shadows of regret.
Young, we move through time slowly.
Old, we watch ourselves decay faster
than dreams play their seductive music,
the tricks of memory. Sudden as black
clouds shadow people from the sea,
they leap into their graves, yet will not
rest there. Chant the rules of sorrow
each night for me. A wren passes over
a backyard garden. A martin's sapphire
plumage dazzles at a window, tomorrow, tomorrow.

Jianzhang

As if intent on something,
all day I watch
through a window
white clouds growing.
It is spring.
Who doesn't appreciate
a happy dream?
My white, shaggy hair
hangs down,
my face is unshaven,
my emerald irises
smile at mysteries,
my parched, pink lips,
pinched and old, smack
like flapping fish as I gnaw an apple.

Huineng

The mind is a mirror.
Polish it. Do not
let dust collect.
Do not mistake
the face you see for it.
The tree of dreams
has no roots or boughs,
its door has no handle
to open it with,
its window no latch
to lock it with.
The only glass
a mirror needs
to reflect your soul
is transparency.
Polish it, I say. Wipe it
clean of steam from your breath.

Caliban

Perhaps, after all, it is solitude that made the world, yet left it undivided,
light, when you consider it, much like dark. Last night,
I watched a ground-hugging fog swallow a whitewashed
half-moon as if hungry, famished for its light,
a comic sight, Sycorax. This morning, mist hovers over bewitched woods
sparing waking eyes a too bright sunrise. I think of you dead,
Prospero, yet still managing to make magic. I have never understood
how you freed yourself from your island. "Sleep is my best friend," you said.
Sometimes I believe art begins and ends
in betrayal, how we delay telling
lies when it is long past time to quit it.
I write you this letter, admitting it cuts deep, rends
my spirit as well, since what I say makes me look to be a liar. I dream. I dream
all my days of beauty, and when I wake from it, from the heartache of it, fit
to be tied and hit as you would do to chastise me, I long for the pain of it again, again
to be back on our island, wrecking havoc, dreaming.

Thomas Traherne

1

Centuries ago, Traherne wrote how tears we've shed
today by tomorrow night might shine for us like pearls.
Darkness can be a boon if you do not dread
its logic, the visions it grants of girls
and boys on summer days rushing over hills,
across farms, meadows, resting in a field
beneath a green screen of tall trees that fills
the horizon with a forest's wall like a shield
wielded to spare young eyes from too fierce a light
seen too soon.
                                        But, after years of tears, is it worth
falling asleep one last time to glimpse the sight
of the sun rising over ivy, vines, and brush
where old men and women still wander as if the earth
had wooed them back to woods where warbler, wren, thrush
once sang to them, in their innocence, of life's sorrows,
how one day each pain they've suffered might shine more lustrous than pearls?

2

The sun is a pale, flat disc bulging on a broken horizon
drifting out of night. Its blazoning light steams
in the gray mist, then flames yellow. Shadows
etch ink-dark marks on hills. The trees'
calligraphy is brushed in ancient ways, each stoke
freeing the mind to see clarity is a way of dreaming.

In the park, a late September summer burns
leaves and grass into an amber
so glassy it looks as if light
is flaking off them like rust. For the fifth day,
heat compresses winds too dusty
to breathe without coughing, the body oppressed
by the seething, pearl white
sky at noon, the shrillness of it, its sublimity
unbearable, the way ahead lit
not for anyone to see it, but for it to be incredible.

3

A moon white chill's in the air. The starless city
sky's lit from below by streetlights, by San Francisco's
nightly glow, its dread of dark, its petty
infidelities, the dreams it repeats down rows
upon rows of houses,
                                        like stories I've told of my-
self, living my days as if I believed in them,
the fictional past, the lies a person goes by
because all he maintains he has been, as at a whim
of fate, is being taken away or is certain
to fall, to fail in the draw of a card, a match
of a game he'll have to quit playing since it is plain
by the odds that he will lose.

                                        There must be a catch,
some way out, a better future I couldn't refuse,
not like this one reflected in the lights of a city
burning for the show of it.

                                        But why must I choose
between a world on fire and a darkening sea.

You walked me to my home, kissed me, then left.
Now you are the one I tell them my dreams about,
the beauty I once knew, sky blue eyes, cleft
chin, a moving man's muscles and grip.

                                                        What doubt
I have is not mine only. I am eyed by a death
that likes lying about me, is my daily enemy,
who is taking my fantasies, my pride, my breath
away
            as you still do, my love, my final unreality.

What remains? My life is failing me, like a tide
on its way out, cleaning the beach, wiping

it free from detritus for another day, the wide
strand white as snow
                                        as if there were nothing
it has left behind but glittering sand, the colorless,
clear white sky, the piercing sun,
                                                        the purity
of a dreaming that is like a gift sometimes, a new nakedness,
the soul prepared, stripped bare
to wear
round its neck,
for all to see,
sorrows' translucent,
costly
string of pearls.

John Keats

The storied masters of gardens dance as flowers bloom, as treasured gemstones open to probing eyes, men, women drinking and laughing into wrinkled old age, their spirits still fragrant and delicate as magnolia in May as if they were white-haired, frail children singing, grieving in their joy-drunk merriment, as if heeding the call of poetry to return to a paradise where, clear and tranquil as a river, the silence of ultimate things flows through the world with the rhythmic beat, the tumultuous pulse of blood coursing through mortal flesh.

Senta

Great storms have long tortured my love. He's wearied of the sea,
a sailor imploring the tempest
to end his torment, to rid his memory
of his too many crimes, to let him find rest
in my arms. I wove at my loom
and sang of my dreams as if to an ocean-tossed,
wind-battered man. Suddenly, he appears in my room,
doomed to wander, to be lost
until the nightmare ends, a new world begins.
But my love has destroyed
what peace I've known. His sins
are mine to bear, we both too overjoyed
to save ourselves, our dreams fulfilled. If wars
leave scars
that love can never heal, what is dreaming for?

Franz Kafka

It's another nightmare night. A crab, turned on its back,
attacks me with its claws and legs,
gulls, ravens hungrily pecking at it
as its twitching body begs
for mercy, a pit
in its belly already slit open by a crow's
sharp beak.
A little girl prods it with a stick, who knows
why, maybe out of curiosity,
then turns it over as if trying
to encourage it to sneak
away, saving itself, to crawl toward a sea
that at high tide has abandoned
it on the beach's black sand, as if an ocean could rectify
what it has done by
disobeying what Law has commanded.

Hart Crane

The dawn star and a half moon die together, alone.
A spring wind whips in off the ocean. The sand,
rippling like waves, pricks my face. What sun shone
through the noon bright sea when he jumped? My hand
seeks his hand. I am also sea-drunk. Overnight,
new gusts have piled taller dunes on the highway.
Far west, it is black where the earth curves, a slight
etched line that cracks dreams open. It is our day.
I slip through time, through space, ninety years late.
And, as I sleep, I struggle to reach him right before
he leaps off a deck of the Orizaba. We would deny fate,
Hart and I, and swim side by side to the waiting shore
of Atlantis as it rises from the water once more, as love will do:
out of the shark-infested seas to reach, look, safe harbor at last and rescue.

Darl Bundren

The war was like home, Mississippi,
unraveling, spilling, a stuck hog's guts
slopping a tub. Ben's blasted knee,
Dalton tangled on the wire, Clay's nuts

blown off, floating in a moon-lit pool,
Leith burning up. It was a Mississippi
rain they died in, a runny stool
of mud the color of sassafras tea,

bi-planes hungry as buzzards. My mother
never loved me. My dad's like God,
feckless, lazy, toothless, more a bother
to his kids than a comfort. I know I'm odd.

No use with tools. My fishing rod
catches nothing. I'm good as dead,
bayoneted. Where's the watch, the gold fob
I bought in Paris? Flies buzz in my head.

Maybe it's a whizbang . Maybe it's time.
Back home, I've got three brothers, a sister.
But I was born in France, in the slime,
the muck, the roiling muddy water

flooding trenches with blood. I like a nice inn,
an estaminet, a glass of red wine,
a bed of my own where I can sin
if I l want to miles away from the line

and listen to the rain on a strange roof
and dream of home and how it's the same
here as there, war the only truth,
the way the world's been made. My name

is Darl. Darl is my brother, too. You are
Darl also, like Dalton, caught, pricked
by the barbs, Clay, balls flung far,
high up, dropping beside me, Leith tricked

into running too soon by the sun. Buddies.
Someone's friend, if not mine. Alone, I stare
through walls trying to see how He sees
the world, even Mississippi where

no one's ever at home and the train
I ride in goes backwards to France
and in the hot July sun the rain
pours up from the earth. Luck, chance,

like jokes, make me laugh. Insanity?
My brother Cash tells me I'm out
of balance. But if flood, fire can't bury
the dead, why not cry or shout

or laugh? At you. At God. At the war
in my head that never stops, won't quit,
that sticks and burns like roofing tar
on Cash's skin. Like cement on bone. I sit

in my room in Jackson, sharp as a knife
I'm told, and hear the lies they say. Be
peaceful, brother. The war, that life,
France is over. You're home. Dream on. It's Mississippi.

Thomas Wolfe

Mine is the youth that is an old man's sleep, mine my dreams of honeysuckle, pine woods, a lake, a cabin abandoned in the war, the images I've discarded–soldiers' photographs, a jar rank with rancid water, ripped pillow cases, yellowed letters, their pencil marks illegible, cracked plates, broken laces dangling from muddy shoes, things from the uninhabited house my buddies and I in childhood
desecrated.

The boy I used to be believed in looming clouds, each afternoon a new thunderstorm, the freedom of summertime, moccasins sliding through water, dew-wet grass to lie on, red clay, limestone caves to hide in, the air gusting warm and strong, the sun at twilight shining through me as through mist, the country it set in, the backwoods, the Carolina landscape I've never quit seeing inside me, cooling breezes in September, the secrets they had promised not to betray me for, the radiant after day of fall's first storm's big blow, the romance that its winds restore, the deserted house, littered with scattered memories, I'd found in woods, transcendently in my dreams to stay.

Antonio Machado

Stay steady and patient, my friend. Take keen note of the tide as it changes.
Wait as your boat in dry dock waits. Don't be overly eager
to return to the sea. Whoever in patience manages
to delay departure wins in the end since life lasts longer
than poetry which is only a game we like to play sometimes. But if life
should prove brief, as it often does, and the sea too risky for the dinghy
or rowboat you would escape in, remain patient despite whatever strife
troubles your days and old ways of believing. Don't go. Don't leave us. Be
hopeful since maybe poetry is what you stay here for, after all,
what you must live near,
by the sea.

But God is not the same as the sea. God is of the sea he chooses to shine
on like moon upon water. It is where he appears, if he does, out of nowhere
like the white sails of a boat silently bound for an empty shoreline.
The sea is his bed, where he wakes up and, in spite of great cares,
falls asleep on sometimes, too. The sea he created is the sea that also bore
him like a mother, matrix of springtime and its storms. He is the creator
whose creatures fear they have created him, yet whose breath is their spirit
forever and ever. Have I made you, Lord, they wonder, as you with your spit
and clay made me? No. But adore him within you whom you've divined. The stream
of compassion, of love in its kindness, is a God who flows seaward like a dream
that passes from one heart into the night thoughts dreamed by another.

Oh Mother,
Father,
torrential rain
is fast
falling from clouds
that obscure you
from all our knowing.
If it must last,
if it must drown us,
let my dreams mean something.

Margery Donna Allison

During the war, I strolled with my father holding
my hand through the moorlands
one morning, desolate and lovely, like listening
to singing in the pub. The world expands
beyond belief where so few trees grow.
In a scrub thicket, not far from a covey of quail,
I spotted a small, young rabbit, head severed by a blow
of a trap a poacher had set. My father went pale
from pity of it. I turned my head away.
"Hungry probably, poor fellow," he said. We were all hungry
then, especially those who worked the pits close by.
There is not a day passes when a childhood memory
like that or some other returns, overwhelming me. I think I know why.
How can anyone survive horror without feeling pity
for the things of the earth that suffer with us? Dreams of its pain haunt me
at night. You know what I mean. It's like at the end when we're made to say goodbye.

Robert Mapplethorpe

The Mineshaft. Westside Docks. Raunch bars. The trucks
in the Meatpacking District. Under the elevated
West Side highway. Desire enlightened
by rituals, how a man's fucked or fucks.
A bull whip shoved up an asshole.
Leather masks. Plastic suits. Chains. Racks.
The body garbed in the role
it enacts to make it shoot.

Black's
life's color, cave-dark its mortality.
Jerking horn-hard dicks.
So many
to long for. Cruising for tricks,
hook-ups, one night stands. Ecstasy.
Passion. Rapture. No more you. Him. Me.

Eakins' naked boys on a rock
overlooking a wooded lake, the lens
left open for a longer exposure. A photo's a lock
on time, men's
dying of pleasure formal-
ized by a camera as the water's
surface breaks.

See? All their borders
are violated. Their appall-
ing beauty, like anemones, calla lilies,
parrot tulips, orchid and leaf in a white ovoid vase.
Outré faces. Who plays
death's part makes love to a thousand beauties.
A head floats above a carved skull on the tip of a cane
a right hand grips. The background's lethal:

black blank pain.

And in my dreams before I die I'd read his note as real
as the photograph he sent me, taken before I knew him.

A curved, black, spindle back chair. A once plush red
cushion faded to rose-soft orange or pink. A pale
olive green sweater draping over it. The floor boards–shed,
barn dark–are centuries old. Tan, like a rusted nail,
two shoes, work boots, laces untied, rest. Ceramic
cups, a bowl for a cat or dog. A chair with carved
arms, the paint worn smooth, no wood exposed. A hutch, thick
slats, built solid.
                                        One door has swung open. It is piled
with stacks of white or gray porcelain bowls and plates.
On its side, the weathered wood of an antique ironing board
hangs from a nail. The ghost of a snow shovel waits
out the glass door propped on a wall.
                                                                                Old things adored
more than lost lives.

The snow shines bright as a flashbulb.
                                                                                So ancient deeds burn
through time.
                                        I promise, he writes. I've just stepped out. I'll soon return.

My Friend Bill

It is shortly past sunrise, but no birds are singing,
not yet. It is cold for Greece, the fog, pale white,
slowly receding to the sea, a bitter chill stinging
his eyes as he stares out far past the rising half light.

Off shore winds sound their own mournful music.
He looks down at his young man's hands,
surprised, no doubt a moment's trick
of the mind, after a man has died, no one understands.

How much the wilds of Paros appear to be the same
as the stormy day he left it decades
ago, only hard weather left to tame
mountains, no more wanton gods, pirates, crusades.

So this is where the end has brought him, to the island
where, it is possible, his poetry began,
to the ancient women, black hair sand-
gritty, exposed skin, clothes filthy, crag-faced fisherman

husband bound to the sea's cruelty, harsh life,
men they know one day they will weep
and weep for, a widow, never more a wife,
silently sweeping the tiered white steps, the steep

paths before the white-washed houses while waiting
for them to return, tragedy's
origins, or one of them, in the common pain
of the daily, primordial, the dream the poet sees

as his own, as everyone's, an old woman dressed
head to toe in night black, staring out, out
beyond sight, far past the horizon, blessed,
alive still, still hoping, ever faithful, ever devout.

2. If Only the Dreamer Could Change the Dream

1

Old friends came to haunt my bedroom late last night,
to confront me for what I should
have long known and never understood, shadows
emerging from the walls chasing after me, friends,
lovers, insisting I make amends, right
the wrongs I did them, make good
my life's errors. Specters struck blows,
hit me like memories attacking me. Life ends
in deepest sleep. I dreamed of flowers, anemones,
columbine, black tulips, ox-eyed daisies lovely
in their white glossy ceramic vases, their various faces,
beckoning me with a French impressionist beauty
until each drooping flower, one by one, spread its petals on my bed
scenting my body where it lay laid out like a cat or snake in the House of the Dead.

2

Yes, dreams confound things.
Nothing is ever clear or right
enough. A thrush sings
high up and out of sight.
A church bell rings. How cruel
their summons sound,
shadows pounding on a window,
the end of a day in school,
bullies yelling in a playground:
childish fears recalling the lies
a boy once told with nothing
he could do or say to rectify
his dishonesty but to bellow
like an animal to an empty sky,
If I can dream of happiness, why not let me?

3

Oh, dark companions of my childhood,
say goodbye as my long life fades
into evening while I say how good
and kind you were sometimes. My shades
are drawn as I wait for the moon to shine
through, not that its light can matter
but the images its gives me are a sign
of a consolation now blurred and softened
to illegibility like love letters you sent I'd leave unopened.

4

A rainy night invites me back to dreaming,
to disbelieving in reality, the sopping earth
steaming after it quits, the summer air
in the woods smelling of sod, oak roots,
spruce, fir needles, drenched brush. A stream,
cut from rock by cascading waterfalls
rushes on. Petals and leaves swirl
in the froth near a path that twists zigzag
to a world l never visited. The aftermath
of twilight abandons me to darkness. Fifty
years later, Kenny still smells good, his sweaty
body tasting of resin and the minty, dense vines
we struggled through to reach the thick woods
that lured us deeper in, but wouldn't let us stay there.

5

A late fall wind sifts through trees grander than redwoods,
bristling, crackling from twigs and limbs whipping
the leaves. Real things are often seen more clearly
in dreams. A jewel-bright stone settled on
the floor of a raging creek, cranes in late autumn
flying home, and Bill lying in his bed denying
his death while I walk past him into nothing, into air,
into clear air as if strolling through a fallow field
I'd once lived close to. A boyfriend I loved only briefly
decades ago told me every dream in the end,
the zero end of each of us, is a creek running
through a plush wide green valley where it turns
into a stream while it gathers tears to grow into a river
that, as it flows, fills itself with all of history's sorrows
until at last it spills into the sea, the bravest, grandest sea
we might imagine while all our nights dream of how not to drown in it.

6

Old man, while you slumber, hike deeper
in or get more lost than you
have ever been before.
Return to one clear place,

never to be a stranger again,
never distant from home,
nothing at the end denying
where you began long ago.

Or wander through twilight
miles out in the country,
far further into the forest
than you'd hiked when young.

Lose your way. Be unguided by sight.
Forget day, the things
you learned there. The dreams
you dreamed will take you

by your arm while a light drizzle
falls through sodden leaves
of holly, rhododendron,
and fennel frail as evening mist.

Lie quiet by a creek. Listen, for
it grieves with you. Study
its book of changes: will o wisp
rising, dogwood, azalea, laurel

flourishing, maple groves on the edge
of woods where shadows stride
side by side and moccasins,
sinuous as waves, slip into a lake black

as the bats that squeak and flap against
winds fiercely blowing down from rocky
peaks you'd dared to climb nightly when
you were a boy lying in bed, greatly loved, safe asleep.

3. Sleepers Awake

1

Flying toward the beach, plovers, sandpipers turn into carved
birds, stone or driftwood figures shadowing dunes.
A foggy morning. Unobserved,
I study the houses around me, lit by moon's
descent, where my neighbors lie dreaming. A thick mist
gathers before first light,
floating like dust in a slight breeze, tiny chips of crystal
dancing in the air. All is good. All is right.

In my reveries, I wait until the sun rises to bless
the eastern hills, let my mind roam
where it will. Time appears
suspended, a lovely, hazy dawn that brings me to confess,
yes, though I have lived for fifty years
in a beautiful place, I dream of awakening elsewhere,
  this world not my home.

2

The sun rises over a brightening valley, a drowsy sun bedded in feathery pillows of clouds. Dawn is rust-colored, dusted with red. An oriole warbles to the sun as if mimicking a Chinese flute, its song wafting through softly billowing breezes that ruffle its tan and ochre feathers.

Then I see an elderly woman waking at first light in the bare bedroom of the cold stone home her husband built for her early in their marriage by a pond in a village in western Connecticut, a frail, lonely widow who is gazing out her window at a garden a next door neighbor tends for her, a sad woman who will not forget her boy killed over fifty years ago in Vietnam.

I knew him. In my dream I call out to him. To John.

Perhaps, however rarely, what we mean by love might be a fantasy in which what we once experienced is recovered from scraps of time, like John's and my last night together. Insects chittering. Tree frogs croaking. Birds singing. One scarlet tanager in particular I recall sweetly warbling by the lake where we used to swim, carefree as boys, but the scene lies elsewhere, too, in western Connecticut.

Confused times I hear and see together even after I have woken up. It is the seventh morning of July in two thousand and twenty two, I am eighty and still feel sleepy from last night's dreams of our love making, lying stretched out on the grass next to John who is staring up at a sycamore while listening to the birds.

My sleeper's fantasies elude me as they will do. Except for this truth. Which I'll try to state plainly.

There is a spirit that dwells deep down in things that might be continuous with dreaming sometimes. Why not call it poetry?

3

A brisk, crackling late June wind, sunset on an evening
so prolonged it stays a golden red
for over an hour, gilding
the air, brightening the white feathers of the gulls gliding over head
to a jewel-like amber. The bluffs at Land's
End blaze. The cliffs behind me, by twilight's intensity,
gleam like slabs of burnished steel mirroring a fire. Who understands
this beauty understands God. The sea
is a lotus-blue, the waves, where they peak, yellow-tinted,
the sand blowing across the beach like pollen
drifting in early spring breezes. A raven
struts on driftwood, black as a priest. Look. My dream survives, reimagined
by light into an image glowing like the rose windows of a cathedral,
sky and earth and you and all.

Terminat hora diem;
Terminat Author opus.

Peter Weltner was raised in northern New Jersey and piedmont North Carolina and educated at Hamilton College (A.B.) and Indiana University (Ph.D.). For thirty seven years, he taught Renaissance, modern, and contemporary poetry and prose in the English Department of San Francisco State. He has published seven books of fiction, including *The Risk of His Music* and *The Return of What's Been Lost*, and twenty books or chapbooks of poetry, most recently *Woods and the City* and *And They Reached Out Their Hands in Longing for the Distant Shore* (Marrowstone Press, Seattle) and *Crow-Black Stones and a Flock of Crows* (Agenda Editions, UK). With his husband of 36 years and their lab-mix Robbie, he lives in San Francisco near the western edge of Golden Gate Park by the Pacific.

Lightning Source UK Ltd.
Milton Keynes UK
UKHW011831260822
407881UK00003B/373

9 798218 049614